Graffiti on the Church

Graffiti on the Church

Ethel Best

Copyright © 2010 by Ethel Best.

ISBN: Softcover   978-1-4500-8219-8
           Ebook   978-1-4500-8220-4

All rights reserved. No part of this book may be reproduced or transmitted in any form or by any means, electronic or mechanical, including photocopying, recording, or by any information storage and retrieval system, without permission in writing from the copyright owner.

This book was printed in the United States of America.

To order additional copies of this book, contact:
Xlibris Corporation
1-888-795-4274
www.Xlibris.com
Orders@Xlibris.com
78678

Contents

Acknowledgements 9
Introduction 11
Brief History 13
Art and Culture of Body Modifications 17
Fashion Styles of Body Art 19
Self-Express 21
Personal Experiences of Body Art and Their Meaning 23
Testimony Regarding Tattoos 25
The Language 28
Tattoo Styles 30
What Does the Bible Say about Piercing the Body? 31
Tattooing Has Witchcraft Roots 38
The Youth Culture and Tattoos 40
One Holy Generation 46
Conclusion 49
Prayer 51
Bibliography 53

Dedication

I dedicate this book to my children Tashell Baker (TeTe), Tonjia Best (TJ), Wilbert Ellis, jr (Piper), my belated son Victor Lamonte Best (Vitto) and my grandchildren Omeka S. Best, V'on Ferebee, Tyon Baker, Victor Best Banks and Amira M. Dunham. Because I chose to walk upright before God and offer him a life of righteousness and obedience, he promise not only to bless me, but that the blessing will flow down to my children and my children's children with long life gevity and prosperity. "How joyful are those who fear the Lord and delight in obeying his commands. Their children will be successful everywhere; an entire generation of godly people will be blessed. They will be wealthy and their good deeds will last forever" (NLT). My prayer is that as Christians, my children will not compromise the Word of God and that they will not be moved by what they see, immoveable in their faith and trust in the Lord. He will cause them to become an over comer and more than a conqueror in Christ Jesus. May the pages of this book bring revelation and enlighten the eyes of your understanding.

Acknowledgements

I must acknowledge and express my thanks to my Lord and Savior, Jesus Christ, for entrusting this message to me and giving me the ability to share it around the world. My family deserves special thanks for their love, support, and understanding.

My thanks goes out to my friend, my sister in Christ, Pastor Mary Spradley who encourage me to complete this book, a message to the world after laying it down for more than a year. Thank you for that extra push and motivation. A special thanks to Jovial Smith for the time and effort she sowed into editing this book. Also, a special thanks to Sean Spradley for exercising his talent in technology in creating the template for this book, thank you, and a job well done. It is appreciated more than you'll ever know.

Introduction

What is Graffiti and is it illegal? Graffiti is drawings or words that are scratched, painted, or sprayed on walls or other surfaces in public places without permission which does not belong to the one that's performing the act. Graffiti is also a form of vandalism and it is illegal when it defaces property whether public or private. To remove it or to clean it up sometimes requires special equipment. Even after cleaning it up there is evidence of the damage left behind. For example, sometimes spots are darker than the rest when removing graffiti. According to the laws of the land, graffiti is a form of vandalism that destroys property. when we get tattoos and body piercings, we vandalize the temple of God which is our body where the Holy Spirit dwells and this is the graffiti that is on the church.

As the body of Christ, we should see ourselves fearfully and wonderfully made in His image. In Psalms 139:14 the chief musician David stated, "I am fearfully and wonderfully made: marvelous are thy works." We are His master pieces and as such the body needs no alteration from man. We are the temple of God and his spirit takes up residence in us. God will destroy anyone who destroys this temple. His temple is Holy and we are the temple of God (1 Corinthians 3:16, 17.) Many people say that they have the right to do whatever they want with their own bodies. Although, they think this is real freedom, they are really enslaved to our own desires. Therefore, we are not the owner of our bodies. God purchase us "with a high price" refers to slaves bought at an auction. For instance, if you rent a building owned by someone else, you try hard not to violate the rules and regulations of that building. Well because your body belongs to God, I compel you not to violate the temple. As Christians, we are free to be all we can be for God, but we are not free from God since he is the maker and creator of all things.

The Body is a highly significant and complex image. Human images and experiences of the body, though under girded by important continuities, are also socially constructed. Ideas of beauty, for example, vary from culture to culture. And the image of the body is deeply tied to particular world-views, in which the body is viewed as a microcosm of the cosmos. The manner, in which a culture regards boundaries of the body, defined first by skin and then, by extension, by garments and hair, reflects the way in which a culture views the boundaries of its social body. The gateway orifices of the body, the eyes, ears, mouth, and genitals may be guarded against pollution in a manner analogous to the way that a nation's ports of entry must be guarded and maintained by checkpoints.[1]

Ideals of bodily beauty may vary from time to time and from culture to culture, but the Song of Songs leaves no doubt that the human body can be beautiful and is a thing to be enjoyed and celebrated in the presence of God, its creator. But the voice of wisdom abruptly draws us back to the practical and spiritual realities of beauty. The prophet Isaiah places the beauty of the human body in proper perspective: "All flesh is grass, and all its beauty is like the flower of the field ... the grass withers, the flower fades: but the word of our God will stand forever" (Isaiah 40:6-8.)[2]

The body male or female is ultimately regarded in the Bible as a physical form with the mysterious capability of emanating virtue and godliness. I Peter, contrasts outward adornment and beauty with the cultivation of the "inner self, the unfading beauty of a gentle and quiet spirit, which is of great worth in God's sight" (I Peter 3:4.)[3]

---

[1] Ryken, Wilhoit, Longman III. Dictionary Imagery: p 102
[2] RVS
[3] NIV

Brief History

The most ancient tattooed specimen is that of "Iceman" a Bronze Age man uncovered after being frozen in a glazier on the Tyrolean Alps between Austria and Italy since about 3300 B.C. The oldest tattoo found in ancient Egypt was the mummy of an Egyptian priest named Amunet, who lived approximately four hundred years ago.

In the third world countries people with dark skin pigmentation generally do not show tattoo well. Furthermore, other body modifications have been practiced for centuries and are still present today. Elongating the neck by adding a series of cooper rings, inserting plated in their lips, and greatly stretched earlobes are just a few of the practices still seen in Africa, Central and South Africa, Asia, and Southeast Asia.

Greek and Roman civilization uses body modification as a form of military rank. There is evidence of tattooing for tribal identification in ancient Rome, as well as, piercing during the first Century A.D. Some Historians believed nipple piercing was used as a mark of rank among the Centurions, a class of Roman Military Officers.

British warriors use body modification as a form of defense tactic. For instance, British warriors stained themselves with woad (blue dye made from a mustard plant): and cut patterns into their skins to psych out their opponents. Some used tattooing as a way to demonstrate which tribe they belonged. Until their reintroduction to the Western world in the late eighteenth century by way of a British exploration of undiscovered lands tattoos remained an archaic taboo.

Cultures with tattoo traditions were converted to Christian religion; their spiritual and cultural rights, which included tattooing and piercing, were outlawed. This banishment of body art stems from the Old Testament passage Leviticus 19:28, which states, "Ye shall not make any cuttings in your flesh for the dead nor print any marks upon you." Those who follow the spiritual laws of the Old Testament let's keep in mind that Leviticus 19:27 states, "Ye shall not round the corners of your head, neither, shall thou mar the corner of thy beard; no tattoos, no haircuts." In other words, according to the Bible, believers who follow Christ should not mark or pierce their body, because you are deforming the temple of God.

In the Military, the custom of sailors and all branches of servicemen getting tattooed continued to this day. Seafaring (sailors) tattoos have roots that go back more than one hundred years. Tattoos were a definite way to recognize one who has died a vicious death in battle. Anyone who has this indelible mark on their body could be identified and sent home.

On December 8, 1891, the first electric tattoo machine was invented by Samuel O"Reily, at the United States Patent Office. This machine was similar to the patent machine of Thomas Edison in 1875 which embroiled fabric. O"Reily's tattoo machine was meant to [4]embroider the skin and his business was the first known enterprise in the United States.

Mid 1970's, for the first time ever tattooists began holding conventions. They came from all over to converged (together) a group to show off their work. Because of these gatherings the course of modern body art was changed.

Tattooing was discovered as fine art in the early 1980's. Artist Tony Fitzgerald and Ed Paschke started using tattoo imagery in their paintings. The interested of fine artists helped not only to legitimize it in the eyes of many, but also, expanded tattooing. With an explosion of styles and imagery, tattooing created a vocabulary of its own that

---

[4] Miller, Jean-Chris. The Body Art Book: p12.
    Lloyd, J.D. Body Piercing and Tattoos: p13

formed a unique trend. This is known as the New School, the period when tattooists began to consider their craft, an art pushing the limits of tattoo technology. Body art is cyclical in nature as you can see from this brief history. The art has been taken to heights never before imagined through the combine technology, historical awareness, and artistic ability. Not just our past, body modification is very much a part of our present and our future.

The revolution of body art had begun. With the tattoo magazines and annual conventions, body modification began to reach millions of people. We see this revolution in today's society with the various types of tattoos and body piercings illustration on people bodies. We see this in all races, genders, and classes of people.

Art and Culture of Body Modifications

Fashion Models with body art and pierced belly buttons are a trend. In Mike Featherstone's book entitled, "Body Modification," scholar Steel states, "today tattoos and body piercing have become increasingly stylish; even fashion models get delicate piercing, and modern Bohemian sport pierced lips, cheeks, nipples, tongues, and genitals." (Featherstone p53, Steele, 1996: p160) Steele also indicates that some believe that tattoos and piercings are associated strongly with marginal and subculture groups that have now become so "mainstream" as to almost be considered "passé") Featherstone p53, Steele, 1996: p 160.) The whole world has rediscovered the ancient art of permanently decorating one's body.

Permanent marks are part of what defines men as human beings. It is a means of self- expression and a vehicle of self-awareness. These two qualities self-expression and self- awareness separates one from other living things. No other animal decorates itself; it is just one aspect of the body art. Tattooing, piercing, and other adornments have been used for centuries in rites of passage, religious ritual, and tribal identification in cultures.

There are emblems that commemorate special events in one's life. Tribes of Asian women shared in tradition of getting tattooed during pregnancy. There were reasons for the tattoos which varied from protecting mother and child against demonic forces, to influencing the sex of a baby, but final result always the same, a permanent souvenir of a life changing moment. This is the reason religious pilgrimages are documented with a sacred tattoo.

The fact that these designs are sure permanent marks, reminds the wearer that they are forever changed. Due to the pain involved from tattooing shows the wearer to be strong and fearless. Tattooing is the most popular kind of permanent body decoration and is considered a respected form of "folk art" created by common people reflecting their condition and culture. Tattooing is based completely on what you are into and think is cool, beautiful, and appropriate.

Piercing is another form of expression that is individualized, creative, and very permanent. You may remove the jewelry but the hole will remain for quite a while. Furthermore, if an individual chooses to leave the piercing out, there's a chance that their skin will have discoloration or scarring.

In the Western Culture, there is a renew interest in tattooing, piercing, and body modification. The Victorian period is a time of public purity and private debauchery. It was fashionable for society women to have their nipples pierced. The children and grandchildren of Victorian women considered the Matriarchs uncivilized. On the other hand, the great grandchildren of these particular ladies did not see anything wrong with this ritual. In the past twenty years "The Body Art Movement" has exploded. It has reached creative and technical heights never before imagined and permanent personal decoration is gaining a wider recognition.

There is a revolution in personal style happening with body modification in silver and gold, self-expression, and fashion. The unique and intimate nature of the body art provides a means to express this individuality, something that is becoming pretty hard to do these days. Certain cultures used body art as a way to reclaim some of the customs and magic of their ancestors. Some want to adorn themselves in ways to show the world something about their personality. There are so many possibilities and variations to tattooing and piercing that it can seem over whelming.

Fashion Styles of Body Art

Tattooing is an expression diverse and dramatic art. Tattooists specialize in certain style. There are three fundamentals styles which are summarized as their basic approaches. Flat is characterized by a lack of detail; traditional and nontraditional, which is known for thick black outlines and solid blocks of color and fine lines, which is distinguished by finer and greater detail.

FLAT TATS

Flat tattooing employs solid blocks for color with no shading, details, or texturing. This type of tattooing is best represented by the tribal style also called *New Tribal*. Simple designs in dark ink has been used to show a person's status, protect from harm, and enhance appearance. One's physical appearance affects his or her self-definitions, identity, and interaction with others. The disadvantage is that it is flat, just a lump of color on the skin.

TRADITIONAL

Traditional and nontraditional acquire its name from the skin art done in the late eighteen hundreds in the Western world. This tattoo is based on clean simple design. Daggers, hearts, snakes, pinup girls, panthers, roses, eagles, and butterflies are all traditional designs. Nontraditional designs are little more cartoons. The advantage of traditional is that they are visually striking and they age well.

FINE LINE

Modern fine line changes the nature of ink slinging. This tattoo looks like it could jump off the body. It will change through the years. It will wrinkle, sag, dry out, and change texture. Flat traditional or fine line tattooing is grouped in a number of different styles[5].

FASHION STYLES OF PIERCING

This style is an extremely popular form of body art. Professional pierces are trained in the areas of safety and health; they have an aesthetic understanding of piercing . . . . There is health concerns you must be aware of beforehand. Most Tattoo experts knows how diseases are transmitted and what precaution the artist must take to prevent contamination.

BODY JEWELRY

Body jewelry is just as important as choosing the right piercing professional. Many problems encountered with piercings even after it heals, result from putting the wrong kind of jewelry in the hole. The design and manufactory of jewelry for the body is in its infancy stage. The most commonly used are surgical stainless steel and titanium. To decrease the risk of infection and allergic reaction, and ensure your piercing heals properly, you must wear suitable jewelry.

---

[5] Miller, Jean-Chris. The Body Art Book: p19
     ibid

Self-Express

Many today use tattoos and piercings as a form of expression, such as turning eighteen, losing a love one, and the birth of a child. Memento mori, or "In memory of . . ." tattoos are usually the person's name, birth, death date, a portrait and sometimes R.I.P. on a head stone with the name and date of death. These various tattoos are placed on the upper outer portion of the arm above the elbow. There are other people who define themselves by joining and identifying themselves as gang members by getting identical tattoos and piercings. The members tattoo the name of the gang or the symbol on their bodies to signify a permanent body modification. This is usually done on the back of the body or the stomach. The language that they use is expressive for example, cholo tears, which are teardrops tattooed around the eye area. Each tear drop represents the life of someone the gang member has killed.

FASHION

Piercing is a trend and a fashion statement for many people. People get holes in their nipples, tongues, navels, and genitals simply for fashion. Body alterations make one very conscious of his/her physical self. The art of tattooing stems from the way other contemporary cultures express themselves, express their beliefs, and mark important moments in their lives with body modifications, which is a fashion trend in today's society.

Personal Experiences of Body Art and Their Meaning

Modifying the Body is a strong statement and an element to the art. Society is affirming and demonstrating temperance over their physical body. Body modification is a good way to hide or camouflage scars, birthmarks, and stretch marks. Just make sure that your reason for wanting to modify your body is pure. Do not make decisions to permanent mark your body while you are angry with your parents, spouse, girl or boyfriend, or significant other. The challenge is to find something that is meaningful to you.

Here are some personal experiences of different peoples' body modification and what it means to them:

Linda, "I got my tattoo four years ago when I first started working at the Villa. I got it just to get it; I was being more oppositional than anything else; trying to fit in; I was at a tattoo party, and it was the style at the time. Today I do not like it. I try to hide it every chance I get. I am self-conscious now. After I got it I did not like it, it was not me."

Mary, "I got my tattoo nine years ago. I got it at the age of eighteen. It does not seem that long. I vividly remember. I was away in college and I wanted to prove something to my parents and I thought it was cool. I still love it and have the tattoo above my left hip it is a little butterfly flying away. The reason I have it is I had a close friend who committed suicide and I decided to get a butterfly as a tattoo and now I want another one on the right side above the hip."

Able, I am fifteen years old and, as soon as I turn eighteen years old, I am going to get a tattoo on my left arm that say, the world is mine's, in old English letters from the movie Scar Face which said the world is mine and everything in it. Because I believe I can be so much good for the world because everybody else is strewing it up."

Testimony Regarding Tattoos

"When I was in high school I really wanted to get a tattoo and a body piercing. So, during high school I got a body piercing (in my belly button). Shortly after I graduated from high school I got a tattoo. Neither action was well thought-out, but more of a spur of the moment thing. In fact, I'm grateful that the man who did my tattoo wouldn't do what I originally wanted. He told me to go home and really think about it until I knew what I wanted and where I wanted it. If he would have done whatever I wanted at that moment, I would be even more regretful at this point. So, I ended up getting something I thought I would want for the rest of my life on my ankle. Now, about five years after I got my tattoo I have a scar where my body piercing was and a tattoo that I wish I didn't have.

I got a navel piercing and a tattoo to be different and cool. After a while of having both, I did not care much about showing them off. It really surprised me in way when people would point to me and ask me about my tattoo. It started to annoy me that when certain people noticed my body piercing and tattoo, I suddenly had become cooler in their eyes. I felt like they liked me more, only after they had found out that I was the type of person who would have a body piercing or tattoo.

Shortly after I got my tattoo, I realized that a lot more people from many different groups of society were getting body piercing and tattoos. The trend of tattoos and body piercings was becoming popular among more and more people regardless of what "group" they were in (i.e. the "rebellious" crowd, as well as the more average straight-laced group of people).

After a few years I got sick of my body piercing because so many people were doing the same thing. Then It came down to deciding whether I wanted metal or a scar. Here's why:

After I was touched by the Lord I was told by a friend that a body piercing and tattoos were wrong because the Bible said so. I was immediately defensive and confused. I wanted to follow the Lord and do what was right in His eyes. So, while I was with my friend one time we decided to look it up in our NIV Bibles for ourselves. We found Leviticus 19:28: "Do not cut your bodies for the dead or put tattoo marks on yourselves. I am the Lord."

We couldn't find anything that directly said you should not pierce your body. In fact, I was surprised to see in certain parts of scripture that women wore nose rings in the Old Testament. For instance, Abraham's servant gave Rebekah a nose ring as a gift when he knew he had found the right wife for Isaac (Genesis 24:34-51 NIV). I believe, however, that nose rings were common in their culture, just as common as earrings have been in American culture for a long time. Therefore, that is not the same reason behind Rebekah wearing a nose ring as someone in America might have today. It would be as simple as her being given earrings today.

I decided to pray about whether it was right for me to have a body piercing and tattoo. During the time I was praying and seeking God about this the Lord led me to Scriptures such as I Corinthians 3:19 NIV; "Do you know that your body is the temple of the Holy Spirit, who is in you, whom you have received from God, You are not your own; you were bought at a price. Therefore, honor God with your body."

I was also convicted by I Corinthians 3:16 NIV: "Don't you know that you yourselves are God's temple and God's spirit lives in you? If anyone destroys God temple, God will destroy him; for God's temple is sacred, and you are the temple."

I felt that I had harmed my body by tattooing and piercing it. I passed out when I got my body pierced and came close to passing out when I got my tattoo. Basically, I went through a lot of pain to look cool. I felt that it was wrong for me to have pierced and tattooed my body, especially because of the reasons behind both-vanity and pride. Between vanity and pride and harming my body that the Lord had created I knew I had sinned. Now I can see that I was not honoring God with my body by piercing it and making a permanent mark on it. Although I was able to remove my piercing, my tattoo is not something that I can just wash away. It is on my leg to stay.

I know the Lord has forgiven me. His grace and love are so amazing, I was living a sinful, ungodly life and then I found the Lord. Jesus died for us all and God raised him from the dead so that our sins can be forgiven and that we may be cleansed of our iniquities. Now, we can enter into a relationship with Him. God did this all through Jesus! The point of this testimony is to share how I was convicted of sin in my life. It doesn't matter what the sin was. We all need to repent and follow the Lord. If we love Him, we will obey Him. John 14:15 NIV: "If you love me, you will obey what I command. I John 5:3-5: "This is love for God: to obey his commands. And his commands are not burdensome, for everyone born of God overcomes the world. This is the victory that has overcome the world, even our faith. Who is it that overcomes the world? It is he who believes that Jesus is the Son of God."

This is the testimony of a young Christian girl who asks to be anonymous.

The Language

Symbolism of Tradition is a good place to start when trying to decide what to put on your body. The language of psych and tattoos are an individual expression.

Here is symbolism, piercing terminology, styles and images of tattoos. The first tattoo that we will explore is the anchor.

Anchors: The anchor represents security and safety.
Bat: Bat symbolized happiness, good fortune, and longevity to Chinese.[6] Bats are most often associated with the forces of darkness in the West . . .
Bears: Bears represented wisdom and indomitable.
Birds: Wing creatures have connotations of spirituality.
Boats: Boats represent the human body, water the path of spiritual pilgrimage and have become associated with spiritual journey.
The Butterfly: The butterfly represents the soul ability to fly away from the body.
Cross: To Christians, the cross represents the suffering of Christ.
Devil: The devil represents the things of the world, which stand in opposition to spiritual enlighten.

---

[6] Miller, Jean-Chris. The Body art Book: p38
Aveline, Erick and Chargueraud, Joyce. Temporary Tattoos: p52

The Heart: The heart is considered the center, a symbol of the eternal soul. It also represents the magnetic attraction one has for another.

Serpents/Snakes: The characteristics of snake explain some of its symbolic significant. It sheds it skin and is reborn, and represents immorality.

Sharks: The word shark means "dogfish mother," the womb that bites.[7]

---

[7] Miller, Jean-Chris. The Body Art Book: p37
Ibid
ibid

Tattoo Styles

Everyday there are new styles and hybrid styles of tattoo designs coming into existence. As the taste and the visual language of our culture changes, the language of tattoo also changes. Death and darkness always have been a classic tattoo. Skulls, snakes, demons, spiders, and spider webs are conventional tattoos. Death, isolation, fear, fascination with mortality, and evil has been taken to another level. This generation has been inspired with fantasy, sci-fi, and horror illustrations, renderings of ghost, demons, and scenes of debauchery (wickedness), and heresy give the wearer a dangerous aura. This kind of work has great depth and dimension.

PIERCING RIPS, TEARS, AND SCARING

If a person should tear or rips their ear it can be sown and should be done as soon as possible. Scar tissues build up and the longer the wait the more difficult it will be to eliminate scared tissues successfully. If this happen you would definitely require surgery to repair.

What Does the Bible Say about Piercing the Body?

In today's society, many people pierce and tattoo their body without knowing the Biblical content meaning, the consequences, and long term affects. Many of the young people in our society are embracing things that seem harmless, for example, piercing the body. The young people are saying that it is a trendy thing to do. Many are showing off ear, nose, tongue, eyebrow, and navel jewelry. Many young people are not aware of the spiritual dangers in such practices. The Bible warns against cutting on the flesh in Leviticus 19:28. Tattooing and body piercing have its roots in witchcraft and the practice of false religions. The Lord made us in perfection in His own image and He admonishes us in I Corinthians 6:19-20. "What Know ye not that your body is the temple of the Holy Ghost which is in you, which ye have of God, and ye are not your own? For ye are bought with a price: therefore glorify God in your body and in your spirit, which are God's." He that is joining to Christ is one spirit. He is yielded up to Him and is here upon possessed, and inhabited, by the Holy Spirit. This is the proper notion of a temple, a place where God dwells, and scared to His use. Such temples real Christians are of the Holy Spirit. Hence we are not our own. We are possessed by and for God, and this in virtue of a purchase made for us.: You are bought with a price. In short, our bodies were made for God, they were purchase for Him. Shall we desecrate His temple and offer it up to a harlot. The temple of the Holy Spirit must be kept clean and fit for His use and residence. We are obligated to glorify God in both our body and spirit, which are His, and we are to honor Him with our bodies and spirit (NLT.)

In I King 18 the story of Elijah about contesting the evil prophets of Baal, a false god of that day whose followers practiced witchcraft. The prophets of Baal were discombobulated trying to get their god to show himself mightier than the true living God. Nonetheless, the God of Elijah proved to be the true God. During the excitement, the Baal worshipers began to disfigure their bodies.

And they cried aloud and cut themselves after manner with knives and lancets till the blood gushed out upon them (I King 12:28.) Deuteronomy 14:1 also warns us against disfiguring our bodies. It states, "you are the son of the Lord your God. You shall not cut yourselves, or make any baldness on your forehead for the dead." This refers to the dead, a witchcraft ritual done to mourn or remember the dead. Therefore where cutting, piercing, and tattooing have its origin in witchcraft practices.

Genesis 35:2 "then Jacob said until his household and to all that with him, put away the strange gods that are among you and be clean, and change your garments; and let us arise and go up to Bethel and I will make there an altar unto God, who answered men in the day of my distress and was with me in the way which I went, and they gave unto Jacob all the strange gods which were in their ears; and Jacob hid them under the oak which was by Schechem."[8]

[9] Isaiah 3:18-23 "In that day the Lord will take away the bravery of their tinkling ornaments about their feet, and their cauls, and their round tires like the moon, and the chain, and the bracelets, and the mufflers, and the bonnets, and the ornaments of the legs, and the headbands, and the tablets, and the earrings, and the rings, and the nose jewels, the changeable suits of apparel, and the mantles and the

---

[8] Amplified
    ibid
[9] The Bible: KJV

wimples, and the crisping pins, the glasses, and the fine linen, and the hoods, and the veils." According to this scripture, this is spiritually dangerous for people, and it opens the door for satanic attack, which allows the enemy to enter their lives. This practice is growing rapidly like wildfire in a forest infiltrating the church. Youth are getting body piercing and tattoos out of a spirit of rebellion against parent's advice. Some men including fathers are wearing earrings to make a statement of their preference by showing that they are macho or homosexual. The youth of today's generation are despising and rebelling against their parents, which is very displeasing to the Lord. Exodus 20:12 "Honour thy father and thy mother, that thy days may be long upon the land which the Lord thy God giveth thee," and "children, obey your parents in all things: for this is well pleasing unto the Lord." (Colossians 3:20)

We are living in the dangerous time that the Bible speaks about in II Timothy 3:1-7. "In the last days perilous times shall come. For men shall be lovers of their own selves, covetous, boasters, proud, blasphemers, disobedient to parents, unthankful, unholy, without natural affection, trucebreaker, false accusers, and incontinent, fierce, despisers of those that are good, traitors, heady, high-minded, lovers of pleasure more than lovers of God; having a form of godliness, but denying the power thereof; from such turn away. If my people, which are called by my name, would humble themselves, and pray, and seek my face, and turn from their wicked ways; then I will hear from heaven, and I will forgive their sin, and heal their land.) (II Chronicle 7:14)

Despite our shortcomings, God forgives us when we are unaware of our action and reasoning. For when we were yet without strength, in due time Christ died for the ungodly (Romans 5:6.) In a sad condition we were unable to help ourselves out of that condition. Therefore, our salvation is here said to come in due time. God's time to help and save is when those that are to be saved are without strength. Not only helpless creatures, and therefore likely to perish, but guilty sinful creatures and therefore deserving to perish. Jesus said, "I have love thee with an everlasting love; therefore with loving kindness have I drawn thee."

There is a generation of young people that love the Lord and yet, do not understand his ways. I believe that there is going to be great revival among the youth of today, because they want a real cause to live or die for. The majority of young people have not seen true

Christianity, and when they do come to Christ many will bring their tattoos, dress, music, and old habits with them into the church. We must make sure that we not indifferent. Nor look down on them, but rather, welcome them, love them, and with a gentle heart, teach them the ways of God. We are called to the ministry of reconciliation. We must be true mothers and fathers to our young people, whether we are biological or spiritual parents and speak the truth in love. We must love and not condemn and on the same token do not compromise the word of God.

Before piercing your body, ask yourself the popular slogan. ***"WWJD"*** *What Would Jesus do?* You would never see Jesus with any body piercing that he placed on Himself. The only scars on His body is the nail that pierced his hands, feet, and the sphere that pierced His side. They were not self-inflicted.

Here is the testimony of a former Hindu who knows that body piercing and tattoos are a form of witchcrafts. He states, "I am from Malaysia and I truly enjoy the overcoming Life Digest. Although enjoy reading all the articles, I find the Little Foxes enlightening and informative. Last Friday, when I entered the GCN chat room, they were discussing about tattoo and piercing (tongue). One of the believers there were telling them it was wrong for Christians to have tattoos. Since I was formerly a Hindu, I know tattoo is from Hinduism and also witchcraft. Also, Hindus pierce their tongue with small spears and pick the entire body with little hooks and go in trances. I have witnessed this personally. But praises God; I never took after any of these rituals even when I was a Hindu. Praises God, I managed to convince a few about the evil of tattoo. One of them asked me for scripture verses, which I promised I would send. But during the weekend, I was busy and also, I couldn't find the relevant scriptures. I prayed to the Lord to help me. Then he reminded me of an article I read in your Digest last year. So I sent your article instead. Praise God for the articles in Little Foxes. Keep up the good work."[10]

Many people are unaware about the truth when it comes to getting body modification and refused to gain true knowledge about this issue. I like Paul in II Timothy 4:2-3a, I have been charged to sound the trumpet; to cry loud and spare not; to preach the word;

---

[10] Amplified

be instant in season; out of season; reprove; rebuke; exhort; with all longsuffering and doctrine. For the time will come when they will not endure sound doctrine,[11] such people refuse to listen to sound and wholesome teaching. Instead, they will reject the truth and rather chase after myths from liberal churches to university campuses claiming to have more enlightenment than their dusty Bible that they hardly picks up from one week to the next. These people do not tolerate the truth; they reject the truth for sensationalism; and they gather viewpoints to satisfy their selfish desires. But no matter how much the truth hurts, we must be willing to listen and seek God's word for the truth, so that we can obey God to the fullest.

When the Lord created man and woman, and placed them in the garden, He spoke these words in Genesis 1:3 "And God saw everything that he had made, behold it was very good . . ." The Lord desires that our bodies be a reflection of His own beauty. When people tattoo their body they are tampering with what the Lord has made. To mark our bodies is unnatural. God's character goes into the creation of every person. We should have as much respect for ourselves, as our maker has for us. The Psalmist David thinks of man, the crown of God's creation, the marvel of the human body, its complexity, its beauty, it's instinct, it's inherited factors, and it's orderliness. As he think of the marvelous weaving of the ligaments, sinews, muscles, blood vessel, and bones, David bursts forth in praise to the Lord, he confessed that he, that we, are "fearfully and wonderfully made, marvelous are your works" (Psalm 139:14). We are his workmanship, his masterpiece, and his work of art. He has created us anew in Christ Jesus unto good works. It is his powerful, creative work in us. We dare not treat ourselves or our fellowman with disrespect, and we dare not alter his masterpiece with body modification. Our bodies are the temples of the Holy Spirit and we are admonished not to defile them. Tattoos on our bodies are like graffiti on the wall, which does not glorify God. I Corinthians 6:19-20 "Why? Know you not that your body is the temple of the Holy Spirit which is in you, which you have of God and you are not your own? For you are bought with a price: therefore glorify God in your body and in your spirit, which are God's."

---

[11] KJV

Why is man so dissatisfied with the way God made him? People are not happy with their features, so they seek ways that will cause them to feel better or for other to accept them. We need to understand that true beauty comes from within not from what we wear or how we may look. When we put more emphasis on the outward appearance we can be ensnared in vanity, rejection, fear, pride, and discrimination. The Lord wants to deliver us from the outward things that we need to feel good about concerning ourselves. When we are in sin we do not feel worthy or acceptable. We can walk in the knowledge that we are acceptable before God, and Christ is our Lord and Savior; we then are free to be the person that God has made us to be without a need to create a different image. People are consumed with trying to be different with body modifications. God is more concerned with how we are living our lives not what we put on our bodies. If a person has a tattoo, it will not prevent God from using people to witness, or from being a minister. God looks on the heart and He can use many things to testify of the Savior, even tattoos. I Samuel 16:7b "The Lord does not look at the things man looks at, Man looks at the outward appearance, but the Lord looks at the heart." In I Peter 3:3 the words written of Peter is the inspire word of God on how we are to adorn, to make ourselves beautiful outwardly, "but not forget the hidden man of the heart, even the ornament of a meek and quiet spirit, which is in the sight of God of great price."(KJV)

Although tattooing has become an accepted practice in our society, the Bible warns us against tattoos in Leviticus 19:28 which says, "Ye shall not make any cutting in your flesh for the dead, nor print or tattoo any marks upon you; I am the Lord." However, just because society approves of something does not mean that it is right in the eyes of God. God loves us, and even when we make mistakes in poor judgment He does not condemn us. God helps us to overcome the consequences of those mistakes. Having a tattoo will not keep anyone from serving the Lord. Anything Satan tries to do us for evil, God can turn it around and use it for our good when we commit totally to serving Him. God takes us as we are and uses us if we yield to His will. When we come out of the world and start serving the Lord with our whole heart and commit to God, He will use you. The past is under the blood of Jesus, and only a hard and unrepentant heart holds us captive to the old life.

God can use those with tattoos who are dedicated, sincere, and who really love the Lord. The issue here is, not whether God can use someone, but rather should Christian pursue getting a tattoo? Just because getting a tattoo is popular does not mean that it is the right thing to do. We should always examine things by the roots and the fruits of the thing in question.

Tattooing Has Witchcraft Roots

In today's society, many people are uninformed of the connection that tattoos has with witchcraft. Deuteronomy 14:1 states, "Ye are the sons of the Lord your God: you shall not cut yourselves, nor make any baldness on your foreheads for the dead." In relation to the dead, this was a witchcraft ritual that was done to mourn or remember the dead. Therefore tattooing, cutting the body and shaving the head is the origin in witchcraft practices. Young people today are shaving their head, tattooing, and cutting their bodies because of witchcraft influences in their lives that they are not aware of. The youth do not realize that partaking of witchcraft ritual can open the door to wrong and defiling influence in their lives. Evil videos, depraved rock music, wicked Internet games, and violet movies are displaying evil trends in order to destroy our youth. Satanic tattoos, skinheads, and other cultic ritual are opening many children to demonization. Demonization (Satanic tattoos) makes it spiritually dangerous. People do not realize displaying a satanic mark or symbol can open the door for satanic attack that allows the enemy entrance in their lives. Because of the spread of false religions tattooing is growing increasingly. The Chinese, as well as, other cultures are covered entirely with tattoos which can make their outward appearance look evil and other tattoo wearers that have small ones believe they are trendy or artistic. Many tattoos have evil and witchcraft themes portrayed as devil faces, skulls, ugly demonic signs, vulgar pictures, etc. which are mostly worn by devil worshipers. It is the spirit behind this compromise that makes it dangerous for a Christian. We who have a tattoo are loved by God. God would rather we did not deface our bodies in any fashion.

There are Christians who object to using Old Testament scripture as a reference to tattoos since the New Testament does not speak of these things. In the New Testament we are call to a higher law. [12]Romans 8:1-4 states, "There is therefore now no condemnation to them which are in Christ Jesus, who walk not after the flesh, but after the spirit. For the laws of the spirit of life in Christ Jesus hath made me free from the law of sin and death. For what the law could not do, in that it was weak through the flesh, God sending his own Son in the likeness of sinful flesh, and for sin, condemned sin in the flesh that the righteousness of the law might be fulfilled in us, who walk not after the flesh, but after the spirit." Romans 10:4 states, "For Christ is the end of the law for righteousness to everyone that believeth." Romans 6:14 says, "For sin shall not be your master, because you are not under the law, but under grace." Romans 7:22 states, "I delight in the law of God after the inward man." Romans 13:10 says, "Love does no harm to it's neighbor. Therefore love is fulfillment of the law. We have the laws of God written in our hearts therefore glorify God in our bodies." I Peter 3:3 states, 'Our beauty should not come from outward adornment, such as braided hair, wearing of gold jewelry, and fine clothes. Instead, it should be that of your inner self, that hidden man of the heart which is not corruptible, the unfading beauty of a gentle and quiet spirit, which is great worth in God's sight."

---

[12] The Bible: KJV
Ibid
ibid

The Youth Culture and Tattoos

Society of today is looking at tattoos and piercings as a norm, instead of a taboo. We see this with our youth and how they use tattoo as a form of acceptance. Parents are allowing their children to pierce or tattoo their bodies. Parents get tattoos themselves and allow their children to have one without thinking anything about it. They seem to think it is the social thing to do. You can buy washable ink so children can make designs on their bodies made by toy makers. This may seem harmless but this is the enemy setting up our children to receive tattoos later on in life. It has been said many times, "I wish I had not been so foolish as to tattooed my body, for today I hate what I have on my body and it is[13] very costly to have a tattoo removed by laser, and therefore I must live with it."

In the following viewpoint from his award-winning book "How stuff Works" series, author Marshal Brain delves into modern process to tattoo removal. By one physician's estimate, about 50 per cent of people who get tattoos later regret them. Before the mid-1980s,

---

[13] Lloyd, J. D. Body Piercing and Tattoos Examining Pop Culture: P.73. ibid

person wishing to have tattoos removed was faced with painful and often scar-inducing surgery. However, the advents of laser surgery, revolutionized tattoo removal. Lasers are not 100 per cent effective; the procedure has become much simpler and less painful.

Elena Gaona states, "Tattoos have long been favored as symbols of identity in gangs. As mainstream culture has embraced the art form in the 1990s, tattoos have become even more prominent among gang members." According to the Los Angeles Police Department, tattoos are now common in gang youths as young as ten years old. Tattoos often reveal gang affiliations. Prison backgrounds and personal experiences that provide officers with important clues in gang-related investigations" in the following articles for the Los Angeles Times, staff writer Elena Gaona explored the significance of tattoos in gang culture.

In gangs tattoos are more popular generally. A gang expert of the Los Angeles Police Department's Central Division says, "Now you see really young kids are more tattooed, at ten years old. That's the current trend. Gang members use to start getting tattoo in their late teens. In recent years, more have seemed to be getting their first ink markings as preteens. Tattoos could give parents insight about their children's activities, I saw a twelve year old who had a gang symbol on the back of her neck, on her elbow, and stomach. Her mother was in denial like most parents."

Many tattoos are based on experiences. The right side of Joey's head has the most personal tattoo on his body. It was a pair of feminine eyes crying, with the words "Only God Knows Why." Joey stated, "My younger brother was shot in 1998. He got shot in Boyle Heights. There were mothers and ladies crying. I know everyone had the same question: Why? That's where I got the idea for the tattoo. Only God Knows Why."

Parental involvement is tricky when teens want body art. Mary Lord, a senior writer for U.S. News & World Report and freelance writer Rachel Lehmann-Haupt explore the mine fields that parents must walk when their teenagers want body art. With tattoos and body piercing increasingly sported by fashion models, pop singers, and movie stars, tattooing has become one of the fasting growing retail businesses in the United States. As body modification has gone mainstream, practices such as branding and scarification that were once considered extreme have become a common place in large cities across the United States. While teenagers are the primary patrons for these practices, the generation gap often leaves their parents feeling left out of the decision-making process and at odds with their own children.

God has a plan to **restore and bridge the generation gap.** We see great tribulation and we see an increased measure of his Holy Spirit being poured out on all flesh. We need to be preparing to function successfully in these last days. Many aspects to the way the glory and judgments of the Lord will be manifested. I believe that God's plan is to restore the generations. *The Call To D.C.* is one assembly that at first was directed only to the youth of the nation to gather in Washington D.C. for a day of fasting and praying. Later it was made a multi-generational assembly, calling for children and parents to assemble together at the Nation Capital. I believe that calling all generations together is pleasing to God for there is strength in unity. God prefers to work within the generations interacting with each other. One of His most revealing titles for Himself is "the God of Abraham, Isaac, and Jacob." He is a God of generations. The righteous declares that their purpose is to declare the glory of God to the next generation. (Psalms 71:18 NIV) "Even when I am old and gray do not forsake me, O God, till I declare your power to the next generation, your might to all who are to come." "One generation shall praise thy works to another, and shall declare thy mighty act."(Psalm 145:4)

There is a generation called by God that obeys his word. Noah was found righteous in his generation (Genesis 7:1.) David's mighty acts are comprehended in the simple epitaph to which every Christian should aspire: he "served the purpose of God in his own generation" (Acts 13:36 NRSV.) Paul exhorts the godly to play it straight, living "blameless and innocent... without blemish in the midst of a crooked and perverse generation, in which you shine like as stars in the world" (Philippians 2:15 NRSV.) The difficulty of living such a life heightens the importance of commending the works of the Lord from one generation to the next.

The introduction of "another generation . . . who did not know the Lord or the work he had done for Israel" found in [14]Judges 2:10.

---

[14] Dictionary of Biblical Imagery
KJV
NRSV
ibid

The only antidote for this calamity is to "tell to the coming generation the glorious deeds of the Lord" (Psalms 78:4 NRSV.) The recitation of these deeds are done with an optimistic and forward looking faith, for it is done for the sake of "children yet unborn" so they might "tell them to their children" (Psalms 102:18.)

God will reward those who obey and keep his commandments. As God hints already in his covenants with Noah and Abraham (Genesis 9:12, 17,) covenant blessing will be poured out upon "a thousand generations" of those who love him and keep his commandments (Deuteronomy 7:9.) This perpetual and exuberant outpouring of divine favor stands in marks contrast to his punishing children for the iniquity of parents, to the third and fourth generations of those who reject me: (Exodus 20:5 NRSV.) No wonder the formula used to express the eternity of the adoration of his people: "From generation to generation we will recount your praises" (Psalms 79:13.) Each generation is called to build on the foundation left by previous generation and all generations are in great need of each other to complete the work that God has called His corporate body to fulfill.

Satan has plans of destruction and we can expect that there will be a generational warfare. Within the chaos and tribulation, Satan has a plan to cause tremendous disunity and mistrust between generations and he will ultimately fail. It is ordained that a great movement in the end times will be one of restoration among generations. According to Malachi 4:5 God said, "Behold, I will send you Elijah the prophet before the coming of the great and dreadful day of the Lord: And he shall turn the heart of the fathers to the children and the heart of the children to their fathers lest I come and smite the earth with a cruse." Even as Satan is attempting to create outright warfare among the generations, the Lord is restoring unity to them, and he is beginning this work outside the church, within the families, ministries, jobs, schools, and etc. God is knitting together multi-generational teams that will fulfill various purposes for His Kingdom. If you are of the younger generation, it is crucial to remember these admonitions in Scripture: "Children obey your parents in the Lord: for this is right. Honour thy father and mother; which is the first commandment with promise: That it may be well with thee, and thou mayest live long on the earth" (Ephesians 6:1-3 KJV.) "Remember the days of old, consider the years of many generations: ask thy father, and he will show thee; thy elders, and they will tell thee" (Deuteronomy 32:7

KJV.) "Remember them which have rule over you, who have spoken unto you the word of God: whose faith follow, considering the end of their conversation" (Hebrews 13:7.)

The older generation gives guidance to the younger generation of today, through love, guidance and discipline with Godly wisdom. There is wisdom in the older generation that can only be received by those whose hunger for truth has forged humility within their hearts. If all you want to do is to defend your views, you are robbing yourself of great wisdom and understanding. Much if what the old generation says is for our protection and good. Let us also point out that holding to the standards of ages past does not necessarily equate with a "religious spirit." There are very good reason for their standards and those who are seeking wisdom will listen with an open mind. There is nothing more foolish than a youth who thinks they have seen [15]it all, trying to correct an elder. Like Elihu (Job's friend) in the book of Job it is better to keep your mouth close until it is appropriate to speak. To the older Christians you must also consider that expecting instant maturity from a young Christian is contrary to the illustration that we gain from watching as human body mature in the natural. We should diligently work to see that Christ is being formed within those the Lord has entrusted to us. Like doctors, however, we must be certain that we are offering the right cure to those who are ailing. Similar symptoms do not always point to the same disease, and the wrong medicine can kill, rather than heal. We must remember that some traditions are neither good nor bad and enforcing them in a legalistic way can be a stumbling block to children, who need the right balance between freedom and law. In Matthew 15:3 (KJV) "Jesus answers and said unto them, why do ye also transgress the commandment of God by your tradition?" In Ephesians 6:4 (KJV) Paul states, "And ye fathers provoke not your children to wrath: but bring them up in the nurture and admonition of the Lord."

In John 10:10 Jesus said, "the thief cometh not, but for to steal, and to kill, and to destroy." He is a defeated foe and he will ultimately fail. I believe that this restoration of the generations is part of God's end

---

[15] The Bible: KJV

time plan that will play a major role in silencing the foe. In contrast to the thief who takes life, Jesus Christ gives us life. Jesus said in the same verse, "I am come that they might have life, and that they might have it more abundantly." Jesus comes to give not to get.

One Holy Generation

In this world today, God is looking for a generation of holy people, which will hear and obey in order for his work will be done in the earth. Leviticus 11:44; 20:7 states . . . "sanctify yourselves, and you shall be holy; for I am Holy . . . ." There is actually one holy generation that God is extracting from all the ages of human history. It is clear from scripture that the entire Body of Christ is actually the same generation, no matter what the age they live in. Consider the following verses written two thousand years ago (emphasis.) "But you are a chosen generation, a royal priesthood, an holy nation, as peculiar people, that you should show forth the praises of Him who hath call you out of darkness into His marvelous light" (I Peter 2:9 KJV.)

Psalms 24 also speaks of this same generation (emphasis):

> "Who may ascend the hill of the Lord? Who may stand in His holy place? He who has clean hands and a pure heart, who does not lift up his soul to an idol or swear by what is false. He will receive blessing from the Lord and vindication from God his savior. Such is the generation of those who seek Him, who seek his face, O God of Jacob. Life up your heads, O you gates; be lifted up you ancient doors that the

King of glory may come in. Who is this King of glory? The Lord almighty, He is the King of glory" (NIV.)

We can see from these verses, that there is a generation that has nothing to do with our date of birth. It is the generation of God's over comers, who have been on the earth throughout human history. This generation transcends 20 to 3000 years difference in natural age. The spirit of God is being poured out unto all generations. From Psalms 24 it is this spiritual generation that usher's in the King of glory. He is being ushered in through a holy generation that has existed throughout all ages. The year of our birth does not qualify nor disqualify us from being a part of this generation. It is the attitude of the heart that matters. [16]Acts 2:17-18 states, "and it shall come to pass in the last days, said God, I will pour out my spirit upon all flesh: and your sons and daughters shall prophesy, and your young men shall see visions, and your old men shall dream dreams: And on my servants and on my handmaids I will pour out in those days of my spirit: and they shall prophesy" (KJV.) The Apostle Peter, applied the above verse to his generation, is part of the same generation you and I belong to. We are the generation that seeks God's face. Therefore, let us make up our minds not to view each other after the flesh, but rather after the life and calling of the spirit within us. Let us deliberately mingle with their generations, yielding to the Holy Spirit as He works out the rough edges within us through this interaction. We need each other, not only to complete the Great Commission, but also to complete that holy work of the spirit that will make us humble and pliable. Keeping to the straight and narrow and yet flowing with the new moves of the spirit.

As the rest of the world experience a greater alienation with each other, and becomes more unrestrained, we must reach out in compassion demonstrating the power of the Holy Spirit. This work of restoration would begin in the house of God (Church.) The world is dying to see this love manifested anywhere. They will run to God who is the restorer of us all. We must live out this call to holiness right where we are, a call truly for this hour, and will be manifested

---

[16] The Bible: KJV

day-by-day– in the lives of the people who want to see a sweeping move of the glory of God.

Isaiah 58:12 states, "And they that shall be of thee shall build the old waste places; thou shalt raise up the foundations of many generations; and thou shalt be called, the repairer of the breach, the restorer of paths to dwell in (KJV.) He wants to repair us until there is not a mar in us until we resemble his love and his glory (TNB.) God is raising up a generation of people that will bring restoration and reconciliation to the world.

Conclusion

In Conclusion, this book has clearly illustrated what graffiti on the church does to the body of Christ and non-believers. I am confidence that God's authoritative instruction through the ministry of his word, spoken publicly through preaching or reading and studying the Bible, or privately through Christian counseling, is the Holy Spirit's means of producing conviction in a believer's heart and give the non-believer's something to think about or consider. The ultimate goal is to bring men into a loving conformity to God's law and to the point that the people willingly agree to the biblical principles establish in the word of God. There are three elements that I wish to convey to those who put graffiti on the body (church.)The first element admonish which is to advise or caution the behavior of their action. The second element is to warn which is to alert, to counsel concerning the consequences of behavior of their action. The third component is to teach which is to show from the scriptures that there is a more excellent way to handle the situation. God is and has everything that you need, or could ever want or hope for. "For God so love the world that he gave his only begotten Son, that whosoever believeth in Him shall not perish, but have everlasting life. God sent not His Son into the world not to condemn the world; but that the world through Him might be saved" (John 3:16-17 KJV.) I beseech you therefore, brethren, by the mercies of God, that ye present your bodies a living sacrifice, holy, acceptable unto God, which is your reasonable service" Roman (12:1.) "Whatever wrong you have done to your body, the temple, remember the words of the Apostle Paul . . ." "I count not myself to have apprehended: but this one thing I do, forgetting those things which are behind and reaching forth unto those things which are before, I press toward the mark for the prize of the high calling of God in Christ Jesus" (Philippians 3:13-14 KJV.) Remember God made us for Him and only He can fill the void in our lives. God longs for us to enter into a covenant and an amazing love relationship with the Him. "You did not chose me, but I chose you and appointed you to go and bear fruit that will last . . ." (John 15:16 KJV) "Before I formed you in the womb I knew you, and before you were born I set you apart . . ." (Jeremiah 1:5 NIV.) "For I know the thought that I think toward you, said the Lord, thoughts of peace, and not of evil, to give to you an expected end" (Jeremiah 29:1 NIV.)[17] In other words, before your parents ever got together to conceive you God had a plan for your life. Your destiny was already ordained and he knows your outcome.

---

[17] The Bible: NIV

Prayer

Heavenly Father, we come before you today to ask your forgiveness and seek your direction and guidance. We know your word says, "Woe to those who call evil good and good evil," (Isaiah 5:20), but that's exactly what we have done. We have lost our spiritual equilibrium and inverted our values. We confess that we have ridiculed the absolute truth of your word and called it pluralism. We have worshipped other gods and called it multiculturalism. We have endorsed perversion and called it alternative lifestyle. We have exploited the poor and called it the lottery. We have neglected the needy and called it preservation. We have rewarded laziness and called it welfare. We have killed our unborn and called it choice. We have shot abortionists and called it justifiable. We have neglected to disciplined our children and called it building self-esteem. Some of us have abused power and called it political savvy. We have coveted our neighbor's possessions and called it ambition. We have polluted the air with profanity and pornography called it freedom of expression. We have ridiculed the time- honored values of our forefathers and called it enlightenment. Search us, O God, and know our hearts today. Try us and see if there be some wicked way in us. Cleanse us from every sin and set us free according to your will. I ask this in the name of Your Son, The Living Savior, Jesus Christ of Nazareth. Amen!

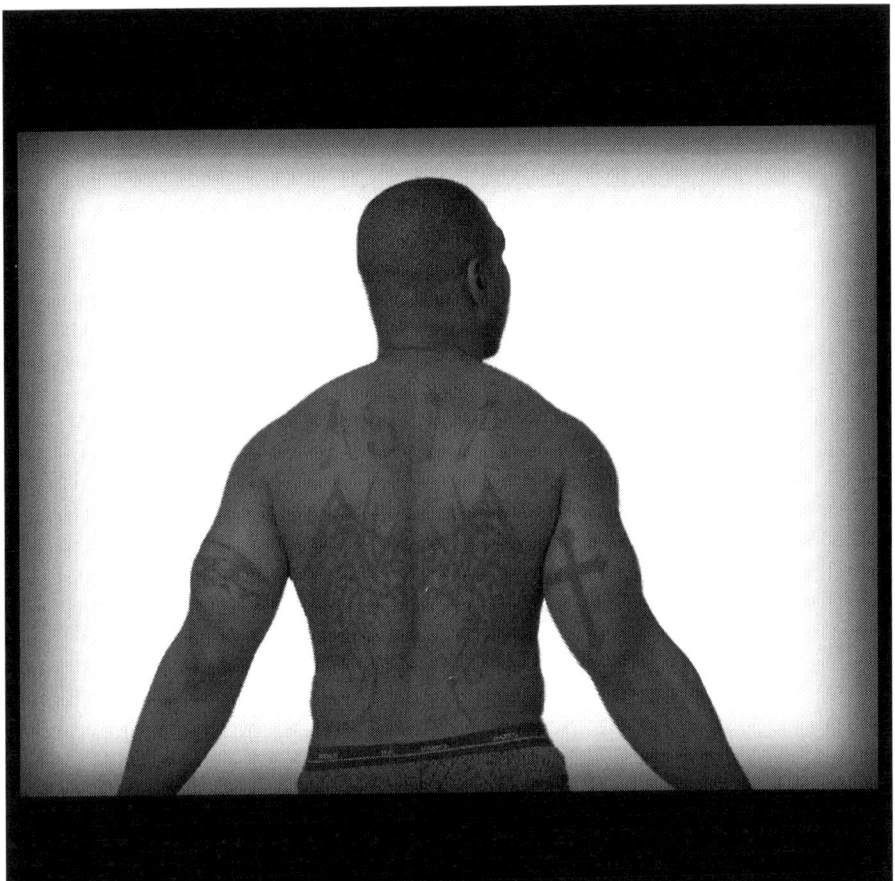

Bibliography

Aveline, Erick and Churqueraud, Joyce. *Temporary Tattoos* Firefly Books Ltd, 2001.
Body Notifications. New York Penguin Group 1997, 2004.
King James Version Bible. Nashville TN Holmes Bible. 1998. Lloyd, D.J. *Body Piercing and Tattoos,* San Diego, Greenhaven Press, 2003.
Lloyd, D.J. *Examining Pop Culture-Body Piercing and Tattoos,* San Diego, Cengage Gale 2002
Miller, Jean, Chris. The Body Art Book *A Complete Illustrated Guide To Tattoos, Piercings, and Other.*
New International Version Bible Grand Rapids Michigan, The Zondervan Corporation 1982.
New Revise Standard Version Bible, "Christian Education of the National Council of the Churches of Christ in the United States of America." 1989.
Rank My Tattoos. *www.RankMyTattoos.com* 10 Nov. 2009.

Made in the USA
Columbia, SC
06 April 2025